The Little Gift Book of the

ROCKIES

The Little Gift Book of the

ROCKIES

Whitecap Books
Vancouver/Toronto

Copyright © 1992 by Whitecap Books
Whitecap Books
Vancouver/Toronto

Text by Elaine Jones
Edited by Linda Ostrowalker
Cover and Interior design by Doug Smith
Typography by CompuType, Vancouver, B.C., Canada

Printed and bound in Canada by Friesen Printers,
    Altona, Manitoba

Canadian Cataloguing in Publication Data
Jones, Elaine.
    Little gift book of the Rockies

    ISBN 1-55110-024-X

    1. Rocky Mountains, Canadian (B.C. and Alta.)
—Description and travel—Views.* I. Title.
FC219.J5   1992   917.11   C92-091024-6
F1090.J65   1992

Cover:
Peyto Lake and Mount Patterson, Banff National Park.
Michael Burch

Contents

Fall colours in the Larch Valley,
Banff National Park.

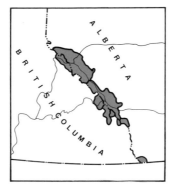

The Rockies

The Rockies rise like a mirage out of the flat bowl of the Prairies. Wave upon wave of peaks recede into the distance, forming a seemingly impenetrable barrier of rock and ice. Two centuries ago, these rugged mountains challenged the first Europeans travelling overland to establish fur trade routes in the far west; to them, conquering the peaks was often a matter of survival. Today modern highways snake through the mountain passes discovered by those men, seeming to tame the wilderness. But winter can still bring blinding snowstorms and avalanche closures on some roads, and the wild beauty of distant meadows and peaks remain to challenge the recreational explorers of today.

Stretching the length of North America, the Rocky Mountains are often called the backbone of the continent. They form the continental divide; the headwaters of rivers that rise in the Rockies flow either west to the Pacific Ocean or east to Hudson Bay. The mountains also have a great influence

Fairview Mountain and Lake Louise
from The Beehive, Banff National Park.

on climate. They act as a barrier to warm, moisture-laden westerly winds from the Pacific, determining precipitation, temperature, and vegetation from the coast to the prairies.

The Canadian Rockies stretch from Waterton Lakes National Park on the U.S. border to the border with Alaska. To the east lie the prairies; to the west the Rocky Mountain Trench, and then a series of ranges that extend to the Pacific. The Canadian Rockies are not the highest of the Rocky Mountains, which range from just over 300 metres (1000 feet) to 4400 metres (14,430 feet), but they are considered to be the most spectacular, with steep slopes, permanently ice-clad peaks, and many glaciers that give them a distinctive alpine character. Scenic areas such as Lake Louise in Banff, the Icefields Parkway, and Jasper have become known worldwide and attract millions of visitors each year. Facilities range from the most luxurious to rough walk-in campsites. Of the national parks, the less developed areas of Yoho and Kootenay draw those who appreciate true wilderness.

In the world of mountains, the Rockies are young; geologists tell us that they were created some 60 to 70 million years ago, when the pressures applied by drifting continental plates caused the land to buckle and rise in a series of jumbled peaks. Long before the period of uplift the area was a huge inland sea, and fossils of marine animals can be found embedded in today's soaring peaks. Scoured by massive sheets of ice during the Ice Age, the Rockies have been carved over time into the rugged shapes that we know today. The glaciers and icefields so characteristic of these mountains are remnants of the last advances of the Ice Age.

Not surprisingly, the recreational opportunities in the Rockies are superb. They range from wilderness hiking, camping and trailriding to simply enjoying the unparalleled scenery. Wildlife is abundant, and bear, deer, elk, moose, Rocky Mountain goats, and bighorn sheep can frequently be spotted, as well as many smaller mammals and birds. Of course, an ample snowfall ensures that skiing is one of the top recreational pursuits in the Rockies, and there are world-class ski facilities at several parks in the system.

Sunset over the Canadian Rockies.

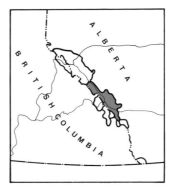

Banff

Canada's first national park, established in 1885, Banff remains the most popular of the parks, with several million visitors annually.

By the 1880s, the Canadian Pacific Railway was forging steel ties between the east and west of Canada, and by 1883, the rails had extended to the formidable barrier of the Rockies. That year, three railway workers stumbled upon hot sulphur springs they named the Cave and Basin Hot Springs. The ensuing battle for ownership and use of the springs led to the establishment of the area as a public reserve, and eventually a park.

Over the years, Banff developed and gained a reputation as a health resort, its dry climate and sulphur baths attracting visitors from as far away as Europe. Elegant accommodations, such as the Chateau Lake Louise and Banff Springs Hotel, were built for the wealthy patrons brought in by the railway. As the automobile gained popularity in the 1920s, the park became less a preserve of the wealthy; this influenced its development and marked the

The Banff Springs Hotel,
Banff National Park.

beginnings of the varied facilities and excellent system of roadways in the park today.

Banff National Park now occupies an area of 6641 square kilometres (2564 square miles). It is bordered to the north by Jasper and to the west by Kootenay and Yoho national parks. To the east are provincial parks and recreational reserves.

For the crowds of tourists who come through here each year, a range of services from the most opulent to the mundane can be found in Banff townsite. In a spectacular setting encircled by peaks, the town is the centre of an extended network of trails and boasts a thriving arts community in the Banff Centre for the Arts. The original Cave and Basin Hot Springs are an attraction for many, but a wide variety of activities can be found nearby. These include hiking, gondola lifts, horseback riding, golf, rafting, and, of course, skiing. Central to the town, and a main focal point, is the castle-like Banff Springs Hotel. It maintains the reputation for luxury established in 1888 when the first hotel was built here by the CPR. Surrounded by magnificent grounds, it overlooks the Bow River.

Possibly the most photographed lake in the world, Lake Louise is one of the primary attractions of Banff National Park. Its still emerald waters, with a milky hue characteristic of glacial lakes, reflect the picture-perfect image of Mount Victoria. In 1890, the first Chateau Lake Louise was built here; the current structure, which dates from 1925, offers elegant and luxurious accommodations.

The townsites are the main attraction for many travellers, but others head out to the wilderness for a true taste of the Rockies. An excellent trail system allows visitors to explore virtually untouched areas in relative solitude. Trails to Mirror Lake, the Beehives, and the Saddleback are popular, and Moraine Lake and the Valley of the Ten Peaks, whose image adorns the Canadian twenty-dollar bill, has long been a destination. The lodge here is a favourite in the fall, when the larches of the alpine area above the lake turn bright gold.

Looking down Banff Avenue with Cascade Mountain in the background, Banff National Park.

The Bow Valley at Castle Junction,
Banff National Park.

*The Upper Hot Springs in Banff are a
popular destination for visitors year-round.*

*The Bow River runs nearly 600 kilo-
metres to its junction with the South
Saskatchewan River in the prairies.*

*Lush new growth on aspens along
Highway 1A, Banff National Park.*

*According to Indian legend, Castle Mountain
is the home of the chinook. Chinooks are
warm winter winds that blow from the
Rockies east to the foothills and prairies.*

*Mount Rundle and the Vermilion Lakes,
Banff National Park.*

The Vermilion Lakes near Banff townsite
are rich in plant and animal life.

A dog team prepares to make a run near Lake Louise, Banff National Park.

The Tower of Babel stands at the entrance to the Consolation Valley, Banff National Park.

Lake Louise was named after Princess Louise, the fourth daughter of Queen Victoria. Mount Victoria (3800 metres/11,365 feet) stands majestically in the background.

*The Post Hotel and Pipestone River in
Lake Louise, Banff National Park.*

An aspen forest in the fall.

*Lake Minnewanka near Banff. This 19-
kilometre-long lake is the largest in
Banff National Park.*

Bull elk near Banff townsite.

The beautiful Larch Valley is a popular hiking area in the fall when the larches are in full colour.

*Camping near Eiffel Peak, Banff
National Park.*

Alpine flowers in Sunshine Meadows,
Banff National Park.

Sentinel Pass, Banff National Park.

Moraine Lake during spring thaw,
Banff National Park.

Rocky Mountain bighorn sheep are found throughout Canada's Rockies.

Fall colours near the Larch Valley,
Banff National Park.

Moraine Lake and the Wenkchemna Peaks
provide one of the most spectacular
vistas in the Canadian Rockies.

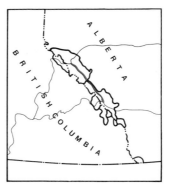

The Icefields Parkway

The roadway connecting the townsites of Banff and Jasper is one of the world's most stunning scenic drives. Extending 230 kilometres (143 miles) from Lake Louise village north to Jasper townsite, it crosses four river valleys—the Bow, North Saskatchewan, Sunwapta, and Athabasca—and offers truly magnificent vistas of mountains, valleys, waterfalls, wildlife, and, most impressively, icefields and glaciers.

Approximately halfway between Jasper and Lake Louise townsites is the vast Columbia Icefield, only the tip of which is visible. Covering about 325 square kilometres (125 square miles), the Columbia Icefield is the largest body of ice in the Rockies and the source of three of Canada's major river systems: the Athabasca, the Saskatchewan, and the Columbia. The icefield feeds eight large glaciers, three of which—the Athabasca, the Dome, and the Stutfield—can be seen from the parkway.

The Athabasca is the only glacier in the park that is accessible by road,

The 230-kilometre-long Icefields Parkway possesses some of the most spectacular scenery in the world.

33

and interpretive programs are offered by park personnel during the summer months. Glaciers are actually moving rivers of ice and can be dangerous, with crevasses, drainage tunnels, ice caves, and ice blocks that collapse without warning. Snowmobile and walking tours led by trained staff offer a safe way to get a close-up view of the Athabasca Glacier, which is seven kilometres (over 4 miles) long.

Even a slight climatic change can affect glaciers, and the Crowfoot Glacier is a dramatic example of this. The glacier was named for its three distinct branches; in recent years the lower spur has receded, leaving just two toes. Crowfoot is one of a hundred or so glaciers that can be seen from the highway.

The largest of the Columbia Icefield glaciers, the Saskatchewan, 11 kilometres (7 miles) in length, can be seen by hiking a short, steep distance to Parker Ridge. This stunning viewpoint is high above the treeline; ptarmigan and mountain goats are occasionally sighted and mountain flowers and stunted shrubs that can survive bitter winter conditions can be viewed.

One of the notable features along the parkway is the many glacial lakes. Glaciers are constantly moving sheets of ice that grind underlying rock into a fine flour-like powder. Meltwater from the glaciers then carries the rock particles into the lakes, where the sediment remains suspended in the water, giving the lakes their characteristic milky turquoise-green colour.

While the sights along the parkway alone can easily entrance the traveller, some of the most spectacular and beautiful of the attractions of this area are a short distance off the main road. About 32 kilometres (20 miles) south of Jasper, the full force of the Athabasca River is funnelled into a narrow canyon, creating spectacular Athabasca Falls. A little farther south, a short jaunt takes the traveller to Sunwapta Falls. Here the river takes a sharp right-angle turn before plunging into a deep canyon, earning it its Stoney Indian name, meaning "roaring river."

The Athabaska Glacier is the most accessible glacier in the Columbia Icefield, Jasper National Park.

The North Saskatchewan River Valley,
Saskatchewan Crossing.

*Beautiful Bow Lake and Mount Jimmy
Simpson, Banff National Park.*

*Atop Parker Ridge looking east towards
the Whitegoat Wilderness Area.*

*Parker Ridge has a high alpine meadow
within easy hiking distance from the
Icefields Parkway.*

*Cirrus Mountain and the Icefields Parkway
from Sunwapta Pass, Banff National Park.*

*Peyto Lake was named for Bill Peyto,
one of the first park wardens in
Banff. It is fed by the Wapta Icefield
and Peyto Glacier, Banff National Park.*

Aspens near the Waterfowl Lakes,
Banff National Park.

*The Icefields Parkway and the Sunwapta
River, Banff National Park.*

*The Columbia Icefield is the largest
accumulation of ice in the Rocky Mountains.
It covers an area of 300 square kilometres
in Jasper National Park.*

Waterfowl Flats, Banff National Park.

Jasper

Jasper is the largest of the national parks in the Rockies, a land of glaciers, rugged peaks, numerous lakes, and the largest ice cap south of the Arctic Circle. The park, established in 1907, covers an area of about 10,800 square kilometres (4170 square miles). From the beginning of its development, Banff was seen as a tourist centre supported by the railways, but Jasper remained isolated. It wasn't until the 1930s, when the Icefields Parkway was constructed, that tourism began to be a significant factor in the development of the park.

Most of the tourist facilities are centred on Jasper townsite, at the junction of the Miette and Athabasca rivers. Once a stop on the fur trade route, then a construction town called Fitzhugh, the townsite developed slowly over the years. Jasper still retains a reputation for being less crowded and developed than Banff. Hikers and other wilderness buffs are drawn to the park's excellent trail system, which has over 1000 kilometres (620 miles) of well-maintained trails.

Like the other Rocky Mountain parks, Jasper boasts a wide array of

Mount Edith Cavell (3365 metres/11,040 feet)
and Cavell Lakes in Jasper National Park.

wildlife. Elk and deer browse on the grasslands in the valley bottoms. In the brief summer, the alpine erupts in carpets of flowers, attracting bighorn sheep, elk, and caribou. Mt. Edith Cavell, known for its spectacular hanging Angel Glacier, also boasts alpine meadows that are among the most beautiful in the Rockies, where ptarmigan, pica, and marmot, with its characteristic whistling call, can be seen.

The Whistlers, one of the most popular destinations of visitors to Jasper, is named for these small creatures. A tram ride to the 2300-metre (7500-foot) ridge affords far-reaching views of the townsite and surrounding mountains. A walk around the ridge will usually reveal marmots, as well as picas and other small animals.

Jasper is noted for its large number of glaciers and glacial lakes. The beautiful lakes surrounding Jasper townsite and along the Icefields Parkway are the result of glacial action. As little as ten thousand years ago the Athabasca Valley was filled with a river of moving ice that gouged deep scars into the young mountains. As the glaciers retreated, the holes were filled with meltwater, creating the lakes of today.

The Maligne Valley is a popular destination for travellers, and another good example of the glacial activities that characterize this park. The smaller Maligne Valley is a "hanging" valley, some 120 metres (400 feet) above the Athabasca Valley. The Maligne River plunges, twists, and turns on its journey through the canyon to join the Athabasca River below. The valley also has other surprises; Medicine Lake, located between the canyon and Maligne Lake, has no visible outlet, yet the lake's water level rises and falls according to the season. In fact, the water escapes through its lower end and re-emerges some kilometres later in the Maligne River. This sudden increase in the river's size is visible past the fourth bridge on the trail to the valley floor. Further along the valley is Maligne Lake, the largest glacier-fed lake in the Canadian Rockies, and arguably one of the most beautiful, with its many forested islands.

*The Whistlers (2470 metres/8104 feet),
with its skytram, overlooks the town
of Jasper, Jasper National Park.*

As well as being the centre for Jasper National Park, the town of Jasper is a busy rail thoroughfare for Canadian National Railways.

*Mount Hardisty (2716 metres/8911 feet)
and the Athabaska River, Jasper
National Park.*

Grizzly bear near Medicine Lake.

Mount Bryce, Jasper National Park.

Maligne Canyon, Jasper National Park.

Young bull elk near Jasper.

Spirit Island and Maligne Lake,
Jasper National Park.

Maligne Lake is the largest glacial lake in the Canadian Rockies.

Athabaska Falls, Jasper National Park.

*Sunset on Lake Beauvert near
Jasper townsite.*

Yoho
Kootenay
Waterton

Abutting Banff on the west slope of the Rockies is Yoho National Park. The smallest of the national parks, at 1300 square kilometres (500 square miles), Yoho is renowned for its pristine wilderness, high jagged peaks, and spectacular falls. Most visitors concur that the park's name—the Cree expression for wonder or awe—is most appropriate.

Road access to many of Yoho's attractions is limited, making the park a paradise for those who seek a true wilderness experience, far from crowds and camera-carrying tourists. Over 400 kilometres (250 miles) of trails lead hikers through incomparable mountain terrain of jewel-like lakes surrounded by steep peaks. Lake O'Hara has become a popular walk-in destination,

Alpine stream in the President Range,
Yoho National Park.

a trek of 13 kilometres (8 miles). A private bus also takes travellers to the lake and rustic Lake O'Hara Lodge.

A switchback road takes visitors to one of the park's greatest attractions, Takakkaw Falls, named from a Cree word for "it is magnificent." At 384 metres (1260 feet) the falls are the second highest in British Columbia.

Immediately south of Yoho is Kootenay National Park, established in 1920. The 1406 square kilometres (543 square miles) follow roughly along the southern highway route from Lake Louise, forming a narrow park that takes in the valleys and surrounding mountains of the Vermilion and Kootenay rivers. At the south end of the park is Radium Hot Springs. Pictographs in the area indicate that the springs were a crossroads for native people long before modern-day travellers soothed their weary muscles in the mineral baths. Like Yoho, Kootenay is primarily a wilderness park, appreciated for the opportunity to see wildlife and to get off the beaten track. In 1985, Kootenay, along with Yoho, Banff, and Jasper was declared a World Heritage Site.

At the southern end of the Canadian Rockies is Waterton Lakes National Park, established in 1895. The park abuts Glacier National Park in the United States; together they form the Waterton-Glacier International Peace Park, established in 1932, the first such park in the world. Unlike Kootenay, which was created around a roadway, Waterton, tucked in the far south of Alberta, is out of the way for most tourists. For those who do make the trek, it is well worth it: the park is one of the most diverse in the Rockies and was designated a biosphere reserve by UNESCO in 1979. Some 520 square kilometres (200 square miles) in area, Waterton exhibits a diverse range of habitats, from prairie to high montane. The mountains here emerge abruptly from the flat plains, and are some of the oldest sedimentary rock in the mountain chain. Because of this diversity, Waterton is well known for its huge variety of wildflowers.

Waterton is a well-developed park with excellent visitor services, from nature interpretive programs to boat cruises on Upper Waterton Lake. A drive-through paddock allows a look at plains bison, and almost 200 kilometres (125 miles) of trails range from an easy walk to a challenging backcountry hike. The imposing Prince of Wales Hotel, built overlooking Upper Waterton Lake according to a Swiss design, has been a landmark since 1927.

Mountain goats, Yoho National Park.

Canadian Pacific freight trains at Field, British Columbia, Yoho National Park.

The Prince of Wales Hotel and Waterton Lakes, Waterton Lakes National Park.

Reflection of Hungerbee Mountain
in Lake McArthur, Yoho National
Park.

Cathedral Mountain (3185 metres/10,450 feet),
Yoho National Park.

*Lake Oesa near Abbott Pass, Yoho
National Park.*

Twin Falls, Yoho National Park.

*Emerald Lake is justly named for the
deep green colour of its glacial
waters, Yoho National Park.*

Takakkaw Falls is Canada's highest uninterrupted falls. The falls cascade 380 metres (1247 feet) to the Yoho River, Yoho National Park.

*Sunrise in Kootenay National Park.
The park was established in 1920 to
preserve canyons, hotsprings, and
waterfalls along the Banff-
Windemere Highway.*

Fresh snowfall in Kootenay National Park.

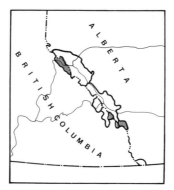

Other Parks

In addition to the well-used national parks, there are a number of provincial parks in the Rockies. Most are far from the tourist track, remote and uninhabited—land set aside to preserve Canada's incomparable mountain wilderness in its pristine state. Throughout the Rockies there is abundant wildlife, but in these undeveloped parks the chances of seeing big game animals such as bighorn sheep, elk, caribou, deer, and moose, as well as smaller mammals such as marmots, picas, and squirrels, are excellent. Coyotes, timber wolves, and black bears are often spotted, as well as the more elusive grizzly bears and cougars. Bird-life abounds and jays are especially plentiful.

Several provincial parks join boundaries with the four national parks, Banff, Jasper, Yoho, and Kootenay. Together they provide a combination of experiences in the wilderness of the Rockies.

At 3953 metres (12,970 feet), Mount Robson is the highest peak in the Canadian Rockies.

West of Jasper, in British Columbia, is Mount Robson Provincial Park. Its namesake peak, Mount Robson, soars to 3954 metres (12,972 feet), the highest in the Rockies. A 22-kilometre (14-mile) trail leads visitors to Berg Lake, from which the sheer wall of the mountain rises 2400 metres (7800 feet). Bordered by Jasper National Park to the west, Mount Robson Park is the source of the Fraser River, British Columbia's longest river. A well-developed trail network allows hikers to see many of the natural wonders here; hikes vary from a few hours to several days.

Tucked between Kootenay and Banff national parks, Mount Assiniboine Provincial Park preserves another corner of the Rocky Mountain wilderness. The splendid 1928 log building built in the high alpine at Lake Magog by the Canadian Pacific Railway is a popular destination for skiers and hikers. There is no road access into the park, and visitors may choose between a fifteen-minute helicopter ride and hiking or skiing some 25 kilometres (15 miles) in to the lodge.

Peter Lougheed Provincial Park, in Alberta, is in the southwest corner of Kananaskis Country, a multi-purpose recreational area set aside by the province. It is Alberta's largest provincial park, at 508 square kilometres (196 square miles), and encompasses large lakes, trails, campgrounds, and both downhill and cross-country ski areas. Fishing and boating are popular on the Upper and Lower lakes, as well as the many other lakes and streams in the park.

A trail leads across the Continental Divide from the Kananaskis Lakes area in Peter Lougheed Park to Elk Lakes Provincial Park in British Columbia. Fishing in the streams is excellent in this subalpine wilderness park, and there is a good chance of sighting mountain goats along the trails. To the west, aptly named Top of the World Provincial Park offers a uniquely beautiful alpine wilderness experience. Many archaeological sites attest to its long history of native use, and artifacts have been found on the summit of 3002-metre (9850-foot) Mount Morro, the highest peak in the park.

Other parks include Hamber, Monkman, and Kwadacha Wilderness Park.

The Kananaskis golf course.

*Yellowhead Lake, Mount Robson
Provincial Park.*

Mount Lorette and the Kananaskis River.

Spring colours near Canmore, Alberta.

*Burstall Pass and the Spray Mountains
in Kananaskis country.*

Meadows near Citadel Pass, Mount Assiniboine Provincial Park.

The Fraser River, Mount Robson
Provincial Park.

*Mumm Peak sits astride the border of
Mount Robson Provincial Park and
Jasper National Park.*

*Storm clouds over the Fairholme Range
near Exshaw, Alberta.*

The Berg Glacier falls from the north side of Mount Robson into Berg Lake.

Mount Assiniboine, Mount Assiniboine Provincial Park.

Photo Credits

Michael E. Burch pp. iii, 2, 10, 11, 13, 14, 15, 17, 18, 19, 20, 22, 25, 28, 29, 31, 37, 40, 41, 51, 55, 56, 57, 58, 59, 67, 70, 71, 73, 74, 77, 79, 80, 85

Bob Herger p. 78

Steve Short pp. 1, 5, 6, 9, 12, 16, 21, 24, 26, 27, 30, 32, 35, 36, 38, 39, 42, 43, 44, 45, 46, 49, 50, 52, 53, 54, 60, 66, 69, 72, 82, 83, 84, 86, 87

Jurgen Vogt pp. 23, 63, 64, 65, 68

Cameron Young p. 81